Noah's Alphabet Garden

By

Randy Arnowitz

Artwork By
FX AND COLOR STUDIO

Many thanks to all the cherished dogs that have generously shared their lives and adventures with me, and to Mark Bennett who helped bring Noah to life.

*Dedicated to
Marilyn Fentress*

is for the
ARTICHOKE
that blooms straight
as a missile.
If Noah doesn't
cut the thing,
it turns into
a thistle.

is for the
crawly BUGS
that some folks say
they hate.
But Noah never
squashes them.
"They're here
to pollinate."

is for the
COMPOST bin,
'cause Noah's
so much wiser.
Instead of filling
up the trash
He makes
natural fertilizer.

is for the
dainty weed
that's called
a DANDELION.
It takes just one
stray gust of wind
to send the
seeds a-flyin'.

is for the EARS
of corn that grow
in the veggie garden.
Pull down the husk
and there's a
worm that says,
"I beg your pardon."

is for the FOREST.
A garden made
of trees.
And when you
go to visit,
Smokey says,
"Be careful, please."

is for the purple
GRAPES
that grow in
juicy bunches.
Noah eats them
for a snack
or after
noontime lunches.

is for the garden
HOSE
that waters lawns
and flowers.
If Noah isn't careful,
it looks like
April showers.

is for the
IRIS plants
with blooms of pink
and blue.
A plant of
many colors,
it comes in
purple, too.

is for the
JASMINE vine
with a scent
beyond compare.
Be careful when you
take a sniff.
A bee could live
in there!

is for the
KITCHEN garden
where sage
and parsley grow.
Noah plants them
all by seed
if he has the
thyme to sow.

is for the rich
dark LOAM—
humus, clay and sand.
Veggies love to
grow in it
and flowers think
it's grand.

is for the earthy
MULCH
of bark and leaves
and hay.
It helps to make
the soil cool,
and keeps the
weeds at bay.

is for
the NURSERY.
It's where they
grow the plants.
Noah gets so
happy there,
it makes him sing
and dance.

is for
the ORANGES
with seeds
instead of cores.
He didn't know they
grew on trees,
Noah thought they
came from stores.

is for the
PANSY plants
that fit in tiny vases.
If Noah looks at them
real close,
He can see their
kitty faces.

is for a fancy plant
that is called
QUEEN ANNE'S
LACE.
Sometimes Noah
cuts a bunch
to brighten up
his place.

is for the
thorny ROSE
who's fragrance
tends to linger.
If Noah doesn't
wear his gloves
he gets an "owie"
in his finger.

is for the
slimy SNAIL
with his house
upon his back.
The good thing is
when he takes a trip
he doesn't have
to pack.

is for his
THUMB that's green,
when he grows
plants and flowers.
It's just a special
way to say,
Noah has magic
garden powers.

is for UMBRELLA
that helps keep
Noah dry.
He likes to garden
in the rain
until the puddles
get too high.

is for the VINES
that grow
around and
up and over.
Sometimes they get
out of hand and
Noah runs for cover.

is for the WEEDS
that sprout
in cracks and
tiny spaces.
Noah says that
they're not pests,
"Just plants in the
wrong places."

Xeriscape's a garden that requires little care. Noah gets his chores done quick with extra time to spare.

is for the
YUCCA plant
that grows when
water's scarce.
Noah's cautious of
their leaves
that are sharp and
somewhat fierce.

is for ZUCCHINI,
when cooked it's
kind of limp.
But leave it on the
vine too long.
And it turns
into a blimp.

ISBN: 978-0-99-864511-7

Copyright 2017 by Randy Arnowitz

All rights reserved. All characters in this book have no existence outside the imagination of the author and have no relation whatsoever to anyone bearing the same name or names. They are not inspired by any individual known or unknown to the author, and all incidents are pure invention. Except for use in any review, the reproduction or utilization of this work in whole or in part in any form by any electronic, mechanical or other means, now known or hereafter invented, including xerography, photocopying and recording, or in any information storage or retrieval system, is forbidden without the written permission of the publisher, Summerland Publishing, 887 Hanson Street, Bozeman, MT 59718

Printed in the United States of America.

Library of Congress #2017932740

www.ingramcontent.com/pod-product-compliance
Lightning Source LLC
Chambersburg PA
CBHW080519020526
44113CB00055B/2524